ANNA X

Joseph Charlton is a writer from the north-east of England. His first play, *Anniversary*, was published in Craig Raine's literary magazine *Arete*, in 2017. His second play, *Brilliant Jerks*, was performed at the VAULT Festival, London, in 2018. He is adapting the play into an eight-part series with the BBC. *ANNA X* was first performed at VAULT in 2019. He is currently writing on the second series of HBO and BBC's *Industry*, as well as co-writing a novel.

JOSEPH CHARLTON

ANNA X

faber

First published in 2021
by Faber and Faber Limited
74–77 Great Russell Street
London WC1B 3DA

Typeset by Brighton Gray
Printed and bound in the UK by CPI Group (Ltd), Croydon CR0 4YY

A CIP record for this book
is available from the British Library

978-0-571-37249-2

6 8 10 9 7 5

Acknowledgements

Jenn Lambert. Joe Phillips. Flo Brockmann. Rebecca
Gwyther. Anna Lavender. Emma Hall. Sonia Friedman. Ian
Rickson. Jack Bradley. David Nock. Imogen Brodie. Patrick
Bone. Mikaela Liakata. Mike Winship. Tal Yarden. Jessica
Hung Han Yun. Sarah Alford-Smith. Natalie Pryce. Angus
Harrison. Hunter Charlton. Craig Raine. Dinah Wood. Jodi
Gray. Imogen O'Sullivan. Isaac Piers Mantell. Eloise
Lawson. Matthew Marland. Becky Paris. Susie Boyt. Rhian
Petty. Rosy Banham. Mickey Down. Konrad Kay. Rob
Murtagh. My parents.

I would like to thank the actors who worked on this script
in an early reading, Elizabeth Debicki and Evan Milton, and
especially both those who developed it with me in 2019,
Rosie Sheehy and Joshua James, and then in 2020–21,
Emma Corrin and Nabhaan Rizwan. I am hugely grateful
to the four of them for helping shape the text into its
current form.

This play began as a co-written project with Catherine
Philps. My favourite lines and ideas in the play are hers,
and I am continuously in awe of her talents as a writer.
Likewise Oliver Rowse who – alongside Memphis Barker –
edited and improved the text many times. Daniel Raggett
suggested the source material of this play and has spent as
long as me working on it since. I am grateful for his
dedication, thoughtfulness, and to have him as an artistic
partner. I would like to thank most Alicia Lawson for her
support, encouragement, and kindness during the last
decade.

ANNA X was first presented at VAULT Festival, in London, on 13 March 2019. The cast was as follows:

Anna Rosie Sheehy
Ariel Joshua James

Director Daniel Raggett
Producer Rebecca Gwyther
Video Designer Mikaela Liakata
Lighting Designer Lizzy Gunby
Sound Designer Mike Winship

ANNA X transferred to the Harold Pinter Theatre, London, on 10 July 2021, and toured to The Lowry, Salford, in August of that same year. The cast was as follows:

Anna Emma Corrin
Ariel Nabhaan Rizwan

Director Daniel Raggett
Set & Video Designers Mikaela Liakata & Tal Yarden
Lighting Designer Jessica Hung Han Yun
Sound Designer Mike Winship
Costume Designer Natalie Pryce

The production was presented in the West End by Sonia Friedman Productions as part of the RE:EMERGE Season, which was made possible with the support of Arts Council England.

Characters

Anna

Ariel

Other parts played by the two actors:

Oz

Jed Grigorian

Carly

Marcus

Conrad

Journalist

Receptionist

ANNA X

because it occurred to me i didn't know what pyramid
    schemes really were
i knew they had something to do with people getting money
    from nothing
like
the person at the top of the pyramid scheme, or more
    accurately
triangle scheme, acquires a number of investors and takes
    their money
and then pays the first lot of investors with the money from
    another bunch of investors
and so on and so forth
all the way to the bottom of the triangle
or pyramid face
which is the kind of stupid thing that happens
if you keep your money in a pyramid and not a bank
    account
although if you ask me banks are the real pyramid schemes
    after all
or was love the real pyramid scheme? i can't remember

                    Hera Lindsay Bird, 'Pyramid Scheme'

Luke is interned and has to appear before a disciplinary council. He uses this unexpected tribune to announce to the world what he calls a revolutionary therapy. His colleagues are horrified: his revolutionary therapy is the programmed destruction of the identity. That's right, Luke concedes, but isn't that the best thing that can happen? What we call the identity is nothing but a straitjacket of boredom, frustration, and despair. All therapies aim at pulling this straitjacket tighter, whereas true freedom means bursting out of it, no longer being held prisoner by yourself and being able to be another self, dozens of selves . . .

'What do you really want?'

'Everything, I guess. To be everybody and do everything.'

Emmanuel Carrère, 'In Search of the Dice Man'

Notes

TEXT

An en-dash (–) indicates speech that is interrupted and stopped dead.

Slashes (/) indicate where speech overlaps.

Speech in [square brackets] indicates unsaid or muttered speech.

When a character's name is listed without text attached to it the character responds without speech.

DESIGN

Lights can change to indicate different places, times, and the movement from duologue to monologue and back.

Video installation or a projector can throw up images, artworks, and moments that the characters refer to – or illustrate locations they inhabit.

The images could be projected directly on to the characters, or on to the walls of the space.

All design, lighting, sound, and music choices are at the discretion of the director/production.

PROLOGUE

Music: Todd Terje, 'Ragysh'. Scattered lights. Unbearably loud. So dark we can barely see. Music fills the spaces in their conversation. We surtitle their words to each other by projecting them onstage. The music's too loud to make out conversation otherwise.

Her HEY

                                  Him WHAT?

Her I SAID HEY

                                  Him OH

                                     HEY

Her HOW'S IT GOING?

                                  Him GOOD

                                     YOU?

Her AMAZING

                                  Him WHAT?

Her I SAID I FEEL FANTASTIC
CAN I
LIKE
LEAN
ON YOUR SHOULDER?

                                Him YOU OKAY?

Her MY STOMACH IS LIKE
MURMURING

I'M ON TRUMP

                          Him WHAT
                     WHAT D'YOU SAY?

Her I'M ON TRUMP

               . . .

             Him WHAT DOES THAT MEAN?

               . . .

Her I HAD A MASSIVE PILL WITH PRESIDENT
TRUMP'S HEAD ON IT

               . . .

                        Him YEAH
                        HE'S BAD

Her NO
I SAID –

                        Him WHAT?

Her DOESN'T MATTER
I LOST ALL MY FRIENDS TONIGHT
    Him EVERYONE IS KIND OF ALONE IN NEW YORK

               . . .

Her THAT IS A MASSIVE CLICHÉ

                     Him YEAH?
                        WELL
            ALL CLICHÉS START AS TRUTH

               . . .

Her THAT'S ALSO A CLICHÉ

               . . .

Him YOU SPEAK REALLY GOOD ENGLISH
FOR SOMEONE NOT FROM HERE

Her WHAT?

Him WHERE ARE YOUR FAMILY FROM?

Her RUSSIA

Him OH
COOL
WHAT'S YOUR NAME?

. . .

Her I DON'T WANNA TELL YOU MY NAME

. . .

Him YOUR EYES ARE ROLLING
INTO THE BACK OF YOUR HEAD

Her YOU SMELL AMAZING.

Him REALLY? I'M QUITE SWEATY

Her EXACTLY
WHAT IS YOUR VIBE
GENERALLY?

Him MY VIBE?
WHAT D'YOU MEAN?

Her I HAVE NO IDEA WHAT I MEAN
I LIKE YOU
BY THE WAY

Him WHAT?

Her I SAID I LIKE YOU

YOU WANNA SWAP NUMBERS?

Him SURE

Her WHAT DO YOU DO?

Him WHAT I DO?
I'M IN TECH

Her TECH?

Him YEAH

Her LAME

. . .

Her DO YOU HAVE A LOT OF MONEY?

Him I MEAN
MAYBE?
A BIT
DO YOU?

Her MILLIONS

Him WHAT?

Her I SAID
MILLIONS

Him WHAT?
REALLY?

Her YEAH
I'M FUCKING LOADED

. . .

D'YOU HAVE ANY WATER?

Act One

Street noise of Manhattan.

Anna You arrive, for the first time, in a city.

You have barely, at all, slept.

But the day you arrive: *you know.*

And not even the annoying couple on the plane –
pretending to hate each other – can stop you thinking:

'America.'

Fuck, yeah.

Ariel You meet people in New York – and you don't meet
them anywhere else in the world.

I met her just after my thirty-second birthday. At an
'immersive party *experience*' on Governers Island.

And, I remember, this girl took my phone and saved
herself . . . as 'ANNA X'.

Block caps. Nothing else.

Anna And in Arrivals, you reflect:

You are twenty-three that month.

The airport smells like disinfectant. You have *really* bad
period pains.

But it is January, sleet is expected, everything is perfect.

And nobody knows you except the taxi driver you just met.

Ariel And, I remember: she said '*Can I unlock this?*'

And she went into the bathroom, and took a selfie. In the mirror.

And for some reason – I dunno why – that was attractive.

Anna And driving from JFK, through Queens, to Manhattan, you are thinking of London.

You are thinking of an Anselm Kiefer opening at White Cube.

You are thinking of a girl you kissed the night before you left.

Ariel Kinda girl you want your friends to see you standing next to.

And being with her, – it was like . . .

Grating a bar of soap.

A box clicking shut.

Y'know? *Satisfying.*

Anna And as the driver talks, you see the city ahead.

And snow is falling – on a cemetery you have already forgotten the name of.

You take your phone and caption lower case.

   Text projected: 'first snow in nyc. kissing pavements, graves, overpass, cars'.

And *truly* – you loved America from when you heard the flight attendant say 'Welcome to the USA, we are so happy to see you'.

You pull up, hand the driver a hundred, and tell him to keep the change.

Ariel And I should say: I *certainly* didn't realise I was gonna be a financial target by my *thirties.*

Very much not so.

And, to be clear – I would never have even *been* in New York – never even have *met* her, had my twenties not been such a disaster.

Anna At your Midtown hotel, you will already be disappointed.

You feel chewing gum on your door handle. The windows are thick.

New York is silent.

Everyone has . . . a dog?

Ariel I mean, I was fleeing the West Coast after a failed relationship, a floundering career and . . . I was trying to *correct* my life, y'know?

Anna You take a shower, pointlessly, at 2 p.m.

You go to Macy's, and buy lip balm from Chanel for forty-two dollars.

Ariel And . . . how I made my money is kind of peripheral to the story, but broadly – I designed an app.

A *dating app*.

Anna And before you start work the next day, you remember your father saying:

'America is for *you*.'

Ariel But . . . this app, okay, was like a club. An exclusive club. Where membership had privileges.

Anna 'That country is built *for you*.'

Ariel With a certain etiquette, a certain clientele.

Anna 'Remember: we are always improving.'

Ariel Which necessarily *screened* applicants.

Anna 'Remember we are *maximum people*.'

Ariel It was called: Genesis.

Anna And the next day you get ready for: *The First Day of the Rest of Your Life.*

2

Lights change. Anna alone.

Anna The first day of your internship, you remember:

Snowdrifts on pavements. Your clothes laid out from the night before.

Versace dress, Prada fur purple bag.

But you decide: *not.*

You choose instead: sportswear from Supreme, rucksack, a coat that does not keep you warm.

And arriving, in Madison Square:

You take an elevator up to top floor 'loft'.

A series of slides during the following illustrating a successful hipster magazine.

The office is called . . . 'The *Institute*'. The last issue's cover is of the editor sucking a woman's toe.

On the walls are Dash Snow polaroids, Tracey Emin light installations, Jeff Koons miniatures. All – the secretary girl says – gifts to the editor.

And there are artists, there are trans people, there is the whole world.

And everyone is queer, and everyone is *just* feeling something *so much*.

You say hello, you are told to organise the mailroom, you are rude to certain people.

You try to eat lunch alone but they want to *know* you.

You say London is very *ahead*, in the market.

And when you swap Instagrams – and they see your travel – they say: you were at Biennale *and* Art Basel?

And you shrug and say you only went to see your parents.

They collect a little.

Ariel I'd just moved to Manhattan.

The city was lit up like a Christmas tree.

Everybody wants to get laid at Christmas.

But: *Success.*

We were celebrating a real achievement.

Genesis had headquartered out of California – to get away from the whole '*SF*' thing.

So we'd moved into bounteous office space in Williamsburg.

The team was growing exponentially.

All we were lacking was investment.

But every day *thousands* were joining an ever-growing waiting list.

And did I dip my pen in the company ink?

Sure.

When girls found out who was behind this thing, they were all over it, yeah.

But honestly? I was disappointed.

I'd met enough girls with eighty thousand followers, who were 'photographers' or whatever – and I started looking for more.

For a real: connection.

3

Anna You hear talk has spread about you across office banks.

And you imagine people in the office saying 'She's not a nice person, though.'

But when the editor pinches your rib early one morning – you know what it is that's coming.

The editor, Oz, is French and obnoxious.

Oz Anna, Anna . . . *Princesse* Anna.

Anna (*to audience*) You feel his hangover, and lust.

Oz (*cold*) Why are you in the mailroom?

Anna This is a guy known for sexting during meetings, smokes in the office, and says he doesn't give a shit about style on a man.

He's just published a five-hundred-page photo-diary of his sexual conquests.

Slides: anonymous torsos with breasts and tidy pubic hair set against beds, cityscapes, in black and white. No heads, with the pictures identified only by their location: Paris, Milan, New York, LA, Buenos Aires.

Oz We go to press Tuesday. You should do the proofs with me. Do you like sushi?

Anna And you 'demur', to use a word you learn that week. You say you will try to arrange for after work. But, he persists.

Oz Lunch. Now. I want to eat.

Anna (*to audience*) And walking to Second Avenue, through snow and inappropriate footwear –

Oz You must be cold, no.

Anna You say *nyet*, to remind him who you are, where you're from.

And as you sit down to eat *omakase*, your breath still steam from outdoors,

He explains –

Oz New York is not the best city in the world. But it *is* the best city for affordable sushi –

Anna (*to audience*) You contradict. (*To Oz.*) Mm, that's not really true.

(*To audience.*) You tell him about St Petersburg, and Putin leading Russia out of financial crisis, and into . . . *the Sushi Years*.

   The editor laughs over his beer.

And you drink beers at lunch, talk, he even takes you seriously. Your knowledge.

Oz *Alors:* tell me what you hate about the magazine, Anna.

Anna Well. It used to be art.

Oz And so?

Anna Nothing. I just liked it more when it was art.

Oz Because why? What's wrong with it now?

Anna Well. Now it's just models, right? Models who look like they're about to have sex. Models who look like they just had sex . . .

Oz So you have a problem with that?

Anna (*shrugs*) I liked it when it was art.

Oz (*beat*) To me, I steered this magazine to being art *and* fashion because they are the same. Sex can be architecture, can be a party, can be an artist. But I take women seriously. Take you. I *see* you . . . You want to be a *businesswoman*.

Anna I am a businesswoman.

Oz *Bien sûr.*

Anna Just not in New York.

Oz Why not New York?

Anna Because New York is five hours and ten *years* behind London.

Oz (*beat – laughs*) And what is wrong with New York's art scene.

Anna It's not new. It's stuck.

Oz *Pourquoi?*

Anna (*shrugs*) MoMA opened a *hundred years ago*. So did the Whitney. No one even remembers who Whitney *is*.

Oz (*laughs appreciatively*) And so what will you do tonight. In terrible New York?

Anna '*Pourquoi?*'

Oz Because I want to take you to the Prada fashion week party.

Anna (*beat*) Sure. I could go.

(*To audience.*) And you try to flirt, with this man who wants to sleep with you.

But this new pill you are on, it *blocks your desire*.

But later, outside your hotel, unlit cabs passing on Thirty-Fourth, high heels in snow – you take your phone.

You filter, square and wait a hundred hearts. And posting, you tag the editor – making your move.

Projection: 'cold? nyet'.

4

Ariel In New York, I was broadly alone.

But fewer distractions meant more work.

It paid off.

A few weeks after moving, we got the call-up from the Grigorian Brothers.

And these guys – are just the fuckin' tits.

I'd met one of them at MIT and he'd gone on to form a Venture Capital firm – extremely dynamic – already with a heap of capital behind it.

And this guy wants to meet at the Havana Room Club – *incredible joint* – at I am not kidding you: seven, in the morning.

Jed Grigorian is obnoxious and American. Tech meets finance: worst of worlds.

Jed Grigorian Eight a.m. starts are for pussies and the public sector. How are ya, man?

Ariel (*obsequious*) Jed, hey – (*To audience.*) And by that point, I assure you: the pitch deck was a thing of a beauty.

Jed Grigorian (*smells the ice coffee he's holding deeply in his lungs*) Don't you love the smell of ice coffee in the morning, Ariel? Like a professional bump of cocaine. *Savour it.*

Ariel (*obliges by smelling/wafting the coffee*) Mm. Fruit of the gods . . .

Jed Grigorian Let's cut to the crap, Ariel: are you a unicorn or aren't ya?

Ariel Well I dunno [about that] –

Jed Grigorian (*stops him*) / Gimme . . . the founder's myth. Gimme the juice. Gimme the naked ape –

Ariel The what?

Jed Grigorian Investment psychobabble.

Ariel (*sceptical*) Right.

Jed Grigorian Pro*ceed*. Tell me how you *package* this. I mean – what *e*-fuckin'-ssentially, is, exclusivity.

Ariel Okay, listen.

Let me take your second question first.

(b) Exclusivity *sells*. We know this.

We crave elitism.

We all want to be unique.

And winning, is also about *losers*.

Soho House, The Yale Club, *Berghain*.

And man – these days – if lunatic asylums had a waiting list there'd be folks queuing *round the block* to put their names down.

Jed Grigorian What's your acceptance rate?

Ariel Six per cent. A slightly harder nut to crack than Harvard.

   Beat.

And (a) our origin myth?

I got this idea – from a *break-up*.

And hey, I tried stuff first. Do *yoga*, try *therapy*, try veganism.

Ten-day no-speaking retreats.

No.

What I needed: was a connection, with a like-minded individual.

And what Genesis does . . . is solve a big problem, for a small amount of people. And gives them a great service.

It's like Andy Warhol used to say about Studio 54.

We're a dictatorship at the door, a democracy on the floor.

Jed Grigorian A safe space for celebrities and creatives to fuck.

Ariel Exactly. But what we're selling here: is *aspiration*. You? Me? We worked to get to the top table. Hard.

And the internet has democratised *overly*. But you know what? People *love* hierarchy. It infuriates them but it makes them horny. It's gold dust.

Jed Grigorian Okay. Let me think on it.

Ariel (*pointing to Jed Grigorian*) And that thinking . . . took all of twelve hours.

Jed Grigorian – Fifty mill for a twenty-five per cent controlling share of the business. Non-negotiable.

Ariel Valuing the business at –

Jed Grigorian Two hundred million dollars. Not bad, man.

Ariel And *man*: I put a down-payment on a Brooklyn apartment with a fuckin' *swing* in the bedroom.

And what was it these guys were even investing in?

Nothing.

No proof of concept.

An idea.

An understanding of how craven human nature is.

Anna And *shakhmaty*, the editor likes your post.

And as your cab pulls up: at New York's newest, *most expensive* skyscraper.

He meets you in the lobby.

Oz La Principessa Anna. New York's *saviour*.

Anna And in a mirrored elevator going up, he takes selfie after selfie of you together.

And arriving, he points out the view:

Oz For *that*, this building is not expensive *enough*.

Anna Points out Rihanna –

Oz Christian Louboutin, Tom Ford –

Anna Says he will make introductions.

And you see girls coming out of cubicles, putting their cocaine back between their phones and cases.

You see car lights reflected in skyscrapers.

You feel like this – all of this – is for you.

Like it was choreographed to happen this way.

And back at the table the editor is praising your taste, your vision –

Oz This girl – *this woman* – is *bound* to be the city's *great new curator*.

Anna Has already told the table your family history, your plan for New York's art scene –

Oz She has the critical *eye* for collecting.

Anna And posted a picture of you on Instagram to five hundred thousand people.

You give him the concept, he fills in the rest.

And later, drunk in a taxi across the city –

Oz Yellow cab *only*. Never Uber –

Anna He tells the driver –

Oz Stop the car, *here*.

Anna (*to Oz*) Why? What are we doing?

Oz Because this building, this place . . . is special.

Beat.

Anna So why are you peeing on it.

Oz You are right, Anna. This city's scene needs . . . *air*. A friend once was going to buy this building. Make it in his image.

Anna (*to Oz*) It's nice. (*To audience.*) And at that moment: you *know* what it is that you will do.

But now – pissing in snow, drunk from champagne cocktails – he tells the city:

'*Mesdames and Messieurs*: ANNA. She's going to be . . . a very *different* kind of star.'

6

Ariel Genesis was *live*.

Thriving.

Obviously, we *had* to celebrate.

It was Thanksgiving that weekend, and fuck were we going home.

The whole company got tickets to an 'immersive nightlife experience', on Governors Island overlooking the city. You had to get a ferry there.

And we're waiting in line to get this ferry, okay.

And one of the girls from design puts something in my mouth.

And let me tell you my philosophy [. . . on that.]

Broadly, I think the trick is to finish drugs by your own bachelor party.

Failing that, maybe your thirty-first or thirty-second year.

And, like, a guy in his thirties – he should have *completed* drugs.

But anyway we're drinking Jameson from the bottle, the mood is *lit* – but then, *I feel it* . . . That *we're on a boat*. Together. And it hits me that I love these people, who've made my vision *real*, that all *collectively*, we are achieving . . . *something*. And suddenly, looking out – fuckin' . . . Statue of Liberty *is there*. And I realise: I am coming up *to pieces*. That my brain *is smoking*.

7

Anna And so: another night, another party.

You've been in New York a year.

You live alone. Company . . . unnerves you.

But you are close.

And impatient.

You look around you at this party of neon crucifixes, and run-down shacks.

They have made this place a waste land.

You push through crowds of people.

And you look up at a high billboard.

It's the name of the night, you hear someone say.

Ariel '*How Did Our Dreams End Up Like This*'.

Inside the club, instantly, I lose everyone.

And the only reason, *I came to*, at this point – even came to my senses – is cos I met: *her*.

Anna appears. Deafening noise again: an extension of the first scene. Surtitles project again above:

Anna TECH?

Ariel TECH YEAH

LIKE

COMPUTERS

. . .

Anna LAME

. . .

DO YOU HAVE A LOT OF MONEY?

Ariel UM

I MEAN

MAYBE?

A BIT

DO YOU?

Anna MILLIONS

Ariel WHAT?

Anna I SAID
MILLIONS

Ariel WHAT?

REALLY?

Anna YEAH

I'M FUCKING LOADED

D'YOU HAVE ANY WATER?

        Ariel THAT'S WILD

Anna WHAT?

        Ariel I SAID

        WHY IS THAT?

Anna I FUNDAMENTALLY CAN'T HEAR YOU

      Ariel WANNA GO FOR A CIGARETTE?

Anna THERE IS NOTHING I WANT MORE THAN A CIGARETTE

        Ariel WHAT?

Anna I SAID

LET'S HAVE TEN

   Outside in the smoking area.

(*Touching/slapping him affectionately on the face.*) Emmanuel. Macron. Come on. *Guess.*

   Anna crouches down near him.

Ariel Uh, Macron . . . On the app? I don't think so.

Anna Excuse me? What?

   Beat.

Ariel Wait, sorry – fuck – I actually entirely forgot what we are talking about.

Anna You are really screwed! *Amazing facts*. Remember! Amazing facts game.

Ariel Oh yeah, shit, you were saying . . .

Anna Okay – Macaulay Culkin.

Ariel Uh-huh. Wait, what?

Anna *Macaulay Culkin is only one year younger than Macron.* (*Beat.*) Isn't that amazing?

Ariel What? No way.

Anna *Way.*

Ariel But he's like . . . the President of France.

Anna *Right.* You got one?

Ariel One what?

Anna *A fact*, OH MY GOD!

Ariel Oh right. I dunno. I'm pretty flipped.

Anna Flipped? Like out-of-control fucked?

Ariel Yeah.

    Beat.

Anna I'm not really like that. I put my pill up my ass.

Ariel *What?* (*Beat.*) *Why?*

Anna (*shrugs*) Cleaner high. Gets in your blood quicker. I feel incredible.

    Pause.

Ariel That's fucking weird. (*Beat.*) Respect.

Anna I'm joking. But – when I was a teenager, at my Catholic boarding school – me and my friends soaked tampons in vodka and put them up our vaginas. To get drunk quicker.

Ariel *Really?*

Anna No that's also a lie.

Ariel Oh man, you're making me look ridiculous here.

Anna It's cool. I'm just playing with you.

Ariel No, I mean – I like it. You speak incredible English by the way.

Anna You already said that. 'You speak incredible English', I know. (*Beat.*) Why do club smoking sections always look like shanty towns? Or concentration camps?

Ariel *Whoaa* –

Anna Or, Ground Zero after 9/11, / y'know?

Ariel Nope, no / I can't . . . quite . . . [get down with that –]

Anna *Grow up*. People . . . *say* . . . things. 9/11 changed the world. It was spectacular. That's the *unsayable* truth.

Ariel I feel like you're cycling through a lot of taboos . . . / [here.]

Anna Yeah? / Maybe I *did* put a pill up my ass?

Ariel (*intense*) No, I'm just saying: what's *your point*?

Anna Obviously I have completely no idea what my point is. (*Beat.*) Damien says 'I sometimes feel that I have nothing to say and I want to communicate this.'

Ariel Who's Damien.

Anna Damien Hirst.

Ariel So you're an artist?

Anna (*shaking head*) I don't make art anymore. I'm a curator. I'm financing a twenty-one-million-dollar art foundation in Manhattan right now.

Ariel O-*kay* fuck. Now you're joking.

Anna No. Buy art, build a museum, put your name on it, let people in for free. That's as close as you get to immortality.

Ariel That your pitch?

Anna Again: Damien.

Ariel Uh-huh. (*Beat.*) So where's your museum?

Anna It's not a museum. So on Park Avenue –

Ariel Mmhm.

Anna – four minutes up from Grand Central there's a building.

Ariel Right.

Anna It has like a Dutch, medieval facade.

Ariel Sounds expensive.

Anna We've raised most of the money.

Ariel You got a pitch?

Anna (*sceptical*) *Why* am I pitching to you?

Ariel Uh because you are talking to the CEO of a company valued at two hundred million dollars. As of *today*. (*Beat, then meaningfully:*) So I am a founder. I make the world. Give me your pitch.

Anna I'm not looking for investors . . . And sorry who even *are* you? I want to look at the light pollution.

Anna lies back to look at the non-visible stars in New York City.

9

Ariel Looking back, several things led to meeting Anna.

The first was breaking up with my college girlfriend – Carly.

We were engaged, actually.

In San Francisco.

She'd been at Boston University, I was at MIT.

And you know those girls that are hot in a Midwest kind of way?

Carly arises from where Anna lay down to sit up beside him.

Carly Hey, sweetie.

Ariel Hey there, sweetie. How you doing now?

Carly I'm good –

Ariel (*to audience*) Yeah that was Carly.

(*To Carly.*) You married yet?

Carly You know I am.

Ariel Kids? You adopted, right?

Carly *Mmhmm.*

Ariel (*to audience*) And that girl, really, should be my wife now. But I can get to that.

The point is, I was at Facebook – specifically Instagram – working in machine learning.

Carly was at 350-dot-org – the environmental charity. Respectable.

But in San Francisco, in 'SF' –

Carly was very *anti* the culture.

Of 'unchecked growth', of 'disruption', of friends of ours going to Burning Man.

Carly *Burners* . . .

Ariel (*to audience*) Of the beautiful, influential people who went out there to find themselves, having already founded a multimillion-dollar tech start-up.

Carly *Founders* . . .

Ariel But the truth is – and this is the heart of it – I FOMO'd to fuck.

I *wanted* to see the orgy tent where you were permitted only with female company.

I *wanted* to try DMT whatever that was.

And I dreamt of being the force behind a start-up that could change the world –

Carly Sweetie, you could start one.

Ariel I know but what?

Carly I dunno, honey. If Mark can do it then you can –

Ariel *Mark Liebling*?

Carly Yeah from frickin' . . . *Phi Beta Epsilon*, or whatever.

Ariel Mark just sold to *Benchmark*. He's a big deal. [He's not even that smart.]

Carly *Right*. Would you want to be him? He's a total meathead.

Ariel (*to audience*) But d'you know what? I dreamt of that.

Carly Sweetie, I thought you wanted to make computer games.

Ariel At school, sure. But –

Carly You know, like that idea you had . . . of, like, *Legend of Zelda*, but in an Americana Western style –

Ariel (*correcting her*) A *Montana*-set Western. *Montana* –

Carly Yeah that one!

Ariel (*to audience*) And I'd pictured a game, okay, where my hero travelled on horse and foot, met maidens on milk ranches, through a vast, *detailed*, open world. He'd bring peace to a besieged community, battling a corrupt county sheriff, who'd summoned a native American god of the dead. And I mean . . . *come on* . . .

Carly Sweetie, I *loved* that idea.

Ariel (*to Carly*) Sweetie, *listen*. In SF . . . people are building *their own* realities. World-altering / concepts

Carly Honey / *you* have ideas.

Ariel But by the time I hit thirty, I realised:

Socially, I was cruising into the stage of life where new people I met were blends of people I already knew.

Workwise? The future was backache, an ulcer, and – what – climbing the ladder to become Lead Engineer? To make two hundred to two-fifty a year?

And, my relationship . . .?

Yeah. I thought about other girls.

I thought about girls reading the *New York Review of Books* on the Metro.

I thought about girls in the Mission District with tattoos from Portland and Astoria.

And at work – at Instagram – my world was bathed in images.

And, in short, I decided to capsize my life.

Carly (*to Ariel*) You left your Nintendo here. And your gym kit.

Ariel Look, I'm sorry.

Carly Are you?

Ariel Honestly? I dunno.

(*To audience.*) But the beginning of Genesis – and my coming to New York – would not have happened had me and Carly not ended.

And this is not some founder's myth bullshit, this is for real.

Toys are preludes to serious ideas.

Necessity is the mother of invention.

I was in Chicago.

On a road-trip back from San Francisco, having recently cluster-fucked my own heart.

Me and Carly had been apart for a few months – okay, maybe a few weeks.

And . . . I went online.

By which I mean – why hide the fact – I downloaded Tinder.

Looking for, like, an introduction to the city.

And d'you know what I found?

Nothing.

No calibre.

A heap of anybodies.

And what I realise is, it wasn't me. *It's the platform.*

It sucked ass.

And I had an idea of an app, okay, that was invite only. Vetted membership. *Prestigious.*

I knocked up the dummy site there. In my hotel room. Circulated it.

In six weeks of getting back to SF, we had a waiting list of just below ten thousand.

In three months, the *LA* frickin' *Times* had run a story on us.

'Genesis . . . The *Illuminati Tinder*'.

And no – man! This is something I built on my *laptop*. In a day!

And was I cynical about it? *Yes of course.*

But Genesis . . . was a business model.

About new beginnings. Where anything could happen.

About making a kick-ass platform, where you felt like you were *getting away with something*. With some*one*. With the girl of your frickin' dreams.

Like Anna.

10

The smoking section.

Anna (*to Ariel*) Take off your shoes.

   She has already done so, or is in the process.

Ariel . . . Why?

Anna Try it. I promise it will be good.

Ariel Honestly my feet feel pretty comfortable.

Anna If you don't like it I will put your shoes back on for you.

Ariel Yeah? Fine.

   He does. Pause.

Oh. Man.

Anna Right?

Ariel S'incredible . . . You are *strange*.

Anna (*tuts*) Everyone in America is very *non-eccentric*.

Ariel Yeah? That's right, isn't it? Why are you eccentric?

Anna I'm not.

Ariel Am I very American?

Anna Yes.

Ariel And you're Russian?

Anna Russian-French. Think that's *neat*?

Ariel It's pretty neat.

Anna You know what I love?

Ariel What?

Anna Getting high on an empty stomach.

Ariel *Yeah?* Fuck I love you.

   Beat.

Anna What?

Ariel I fucking love you that you say that.

Anna Okay. Really.

Ariel Completely.

Anna You are high.

Ariel Yes.

Anna Wanna see my tits?

Ariel What? Fuck. Yeah.

Anna Not here.

11

Ariel I woke up . . . in my apartment.

Two, three hours sleep, around 8 a.m.

What we called at college:

'Drinker's Dawn'.

And the night before, I had been – mark my words: *college-fucked.*

And, I remember, I had a piss so long . . . it was like *the soul leaving the body.*

Anna You wake up and read about his app.

iPhone only. Instagram required.

Download.

Ariel I had a squash game, that afternoon, which I cancelled.

I drank a ton of coffee, which made me uneasy, and online I learnt everything about this girl.

I read the runes.

Anna One hour.

You are accepted.

Ariel Her Instagram was *lit.*

Anna You see . . .

Ariel Into travel, fashion, but funny.

Anna The owner of Box nightclub.

A thousand Instagram models.

Ariel *New Yorker* cartoons, memes that were not dumb.

Anna Influencers, 'photographers'.

Ariel And one of those hundred or so people that only exist in New York's nightlife.

                                        Anna You research him.

Ariel Whose life you cannot believe.

                        Anna His life – like yours – is painted online.

Ariel At private views in Chelsea.

                   Anna A guy not invited to parties at high school.

Ariel At a Peruvian restaurant just opened on Lexington and Third.

                 Anna A guy trying to turn the whole world on,
                                                   for a moment.

                             A guy trying to live his 'best life'.

                                   And you decide: meet.

Ariel Right off the bat, I WhatsApp her.

And through my anxiety, I send an articulate and humorous summary of the night before, the uniqueness of my hangover, and a topical aside about US–Russia relations.

I wait.

Nothing.

And I spent the remainder of that weekend: *dooming out*. Scrutinising that message and hating myself comprehensively.

I take Monday off to deal with my spiralling comedown – no reply.

And man, I only went to the office Tuesday cos there's apparently a 'minor snafu' with programming.

The offices of Genesis. Marcus is a junior tech-bro. Recently out of college vibe.

35

Marcus Dude. Yo.

Ariel (*to audience*) Marcus, our new ML engineer, who we *had* to hire cos he's the nephew of someone at Grigorian Brothers.

Marcus El Capitano. How's it hanging.

Ariel (*to Marcus*) Yeah fine. (*To audience.*) And this guy is a dumbass Princeton Business major. He's been in private equity, he's been at code-camp to retool himself. Now probably on his *sixth* career, age twenty-six.

Marcus Legendary party. If that's working on Thanksgiving, give it to me. Every damn *day*.

Ariel (*to audience*) Spends very little time on his job, all day on client engineering: i.e. checking out girls applying, macking on them.

Marcus Looked pretty jacked when I saw you, man. Awesomeballs. Think we all were.

Ariel (*quiet infuriation*) Yeah. So what's the problem, Marcus?

Marcus Oh. Man. It's minor. Bottleneck issue with membership. Recalibrated pronto.

Ariel (*clearly the wrong word technically*) *Recalibrated?*

Marcus Not your issue. Waiting on update. (*Impressed.*) Also dude, last night – that girl –

Ariel What.

Marcus Nice.

Ariel Y'know her?

Marcus *Yes*. Wait, you didn't?

Ariel No.

Marcus Dude. Kudos.

Ariel What d'you know about her.

Marcus . . . Man, from what I *hear* . . . She's one of those rich art girls who's, like, *elegantly wasted* all the time, y'know?

Ariel Wait, shut up. Will you see if she's on?

Marcus Yeah.

Ariel No I mean like can you check now?

Marcus Yeah dude of course she's on. I vetted her yesterday.

Ariel I send Marcus home to jerk off.

And sitting in the twilight of the office, alone, I open the app. Search. And bam. Right *there*. Swipe to connect. Pending. And just as I am, like – you *doofus*, this girl already ghosted . . .

Connected.

I open a beer.

12

Anna is at a private view with an empty glass in her hand.

Anna Pace Gallery. East Fifty-Seventh. Looking at work by a new artist you're interested in.

You are considering smoking, you are considering leaving

When:

Notification. Genesis.

Ariel Lieven wants to connect.

An instant message conversation:

Ariel Hey

Anna Hi

Sorry only just replying to this

Anna is typing.

Just had a round on

A round on?

Ton

on*

Sorry

Predictive

How are you

Great

How are you

Still feeling it tbh

From weekend

Still at work but

back on it tonight

2 Brooklyns down

Yeah?

Strong

I'm good

Me too

Just got to this art thing

Driving too

38

DRINKING

!

lol

Not driving

> lol
>
> Hope not driving too far
>
> Do you wanna meet?

Pause. Ariel waits, nervously, sucks his teeth.

> (*To himself, not phone.*) Fuck . . . the fuck. So *eager* –
@@)@)(9@

> (*Slowly.*) question . . . mark?

Sorry

exclamation mark

pocket dial

I'm drunk

Slightly

lol

> lol

You wanna meet now?

> (*Not laughing.*) laughing

I was actually gonna say

> Sure
>
> If that's cool?

You should come here

> Yesh

                                              Yeah*

                                              RIGHT

To Pace

Where I am

If you want

                                              Great

                                              Amazing

So see you?

Soon?

                                              Perfect

ok

X

Ariel (*to audience*) I get a cab, from the office, up Sixth Avenue.

My art knowledge . . . is patchy. Okay – poor.

Traffic is horrible.

I google the artist.

Chinese. Difficult name.

He doesn't even have a Wikipedia.

Anna You know when you're aware that you're the centre of attention? That you're powering the fact anyone is even *being there*? . . . or *trying*?

You are with a group of three guys from the gallery, showing off.

Being provocative. Overly smoking. Overusing the word 'cunt'.

Ariel 'No, I'm not on the list, but please let me in.'

'Who do you know?'

'Anna.'

'Everyone knows Anna.'

Anna Inside, everyone is rude.

You know the girls that survive on tapas and cocaine?

And amazingly, you are *looking forward* to seeing him.

Ariel Hey.

Anna Hi. I'm drunk. Wanna get drunker with me.

Ariel . . . Definitely.

Anna In Russia, we have a word for drunkenness more than two days.

Ariel Yeah?

Anna *Zapoy.*

Ariel Zapoy. Nice. (*Beat.*) Should we be looking at the art?

Anna (*shrugs*) If you like.

Ariel Is everyone a dick at this gallery?

Anna Is likely. (*Re: the art.*) What d'you think?

They turn away from us, facing the art.

Ariel Yeah. I rate his content.

Anna Content?

Ariel It's cool. Lotta paint. Reminds me of . . . Roth cow.

Anna Roth . . . *ko*?

Ariel Rothko. Right?

Anna Sure. Why not.

Ariel No? Wait, it says something by the side.

'If I am to paint, I will paint the passage of time itself . . . which concerns the essence of my life.'

(*Nodding.*) Mm . . . yes . . .

Anna (*helping*) – I think it means – in parts of China, like where the artist is from – people buy a coffin when they're sixty. And then they keep it at home and paint a layer of colour on it, every year. Until, y'know, they die.

Ariel Morbid. (*Beat.*) Great knowledge.

Anna I read it on *artnet* in my taxi.

Ariel Man. Wish I knew how to use Google.

She looks at him.

Anna You know: you're almost funny, in a lame geek way? (*To audience.*) And what the fuck: you mean it?

Ariel Thanks. So: artnet?

Anna Mm-hm. That's how easy it is. To get away with it.

Ariel So this guy's brand is like –

Anna Memento mori.

Ariel Yes.

Anna Remember you die.

Ariel Zapoy.

Anna Exactly.

Ariel (*to audience*) And man, *this is flying*. And I'm like:

(*To Anna.*) D'you actually wanna get outta here? Like to a bar?

(*To audience, impressed.*) And she says –

Anna Let's go to *a hotel*.

Ariel (*to audience*) And you're like: What? That's *crazy* – my apartment is over the river. But I'm also like: That would be *baller*.

Anna (*to audience*) And you think, are you doing this? Really?

Ariel (*to audience*) She takes our wineglasses and we leave, onto the street. Like *Rihanna*. And in a cab flying direct down FDR, with the driver playing bhangra, she says –

Anna Play louder, please.

Ariel And by time we get to the Beekman –

Anna You take him to the hotel bar –

Ariel Plush furniture. Chandeliers. I go to the men's. For whatever reason – the urinals are filled *with ice*.

And when I get back, she'd ordered – ingeniously –

Anna (*to barman*) Vodka and grapefruit juice.

Ariel And: it wasn't like I was looking for some . . . whirlwind romance or something.

But I was looking for something –

Different.

Like,

More life than life.

Like drugs.

When going to the store, going for a walk – everything feels . . . meaningful.

Anna And on the way to the room, you think: you are in love with this feeling. Of being spontaneous and reckless and pointless.

Ariel Let's order room service on the bed and watch television.

Anna And it's doubly perfect because he wants to be silly and not just worship my body. (And I *want* him to worship my body.)

I want to get into a bathrobe and tell him, seriously, this will pass but it is fun.

Ariel I am drunk, and completely unavailable to have sex at this time.

I want to look at her – face on, in the bed – and ask her everything about her life.

Anna Wanna play a game?

Ariel Yes.

Anna You think of a word and I'll think of the next.

Ariel Shall I go first or you?

Anna Me . . . When.

Ariel You

Anna *Came.*

Ariel In . . . ?

Anna – *to.*

Ariel My.

Anna BED.

Slight pause.

Ariel Comma?

Anna nodding quickly, excitedly.

Anna I.

Ariel (*thinks*) Knew . . .?

Anna – That.

Ariel It.

Anna – Would.

Ariel Be.

Anna pauses, thinks.

Anna . . . *Alarming.*

Ariel screws up his face.

Ariel *Really?*

Anna Maybe! Why not? Quite good sentence, right? Period.

Ariel You are weird but nice.

Anna You don't know that.

Ariel Okay, but how much can you ever know a person, right?

Anna *That* is a cliché. (*Beat.*) I have no idea what you think of me.

13

Ariel Imagine waking up in a luxury hotel suite.

On a Wednesday morning.

No idea of the time.

Imagine light flooding through the window, dawn chorus of garbage trucks, traffic, and the room being entirely empty.

Imagine collecting your belongings, trying not to smell your own breath, and heading to reception.

Receptionist How did you enjoy your stay, sir?

Ariel Oh, very much.

Receptionist Excellent. I understand Miss Brunel had to leave early for an art fair in Prague.

Ariel She did?

Receptionist Sir, we understand you're happy to collect the bill.

Ariel I see.

Receptionist How would you like to pay today, sir?

Ariel Er . . . American Express?

Receptionist Excellent, sir. To cover Miss Brunel's stay the charge is nineteen thousand seven hundred and fifty-five dollars.

14

Ariel And d'you know what?

Pause.

That was cool.

Beat.

Sexy. Weird. Astonishing.

And I was not so much worried that I'd been robbed –

As I'd been rinsed by a rich girl, who had so much money she didn't even keep track of it.

'Are we seeing each other again or what?'

Instant message sound.

Anna Hey!

Yeah!

have to travel but love to when I'm back

Ariel Right.

Actually?

Instant message sound.

Act Two

Anna, alone.

Anna Time passes.

Winter to spring, the miracle of new things.

Your visa – by coming and going.

And back from London Fashion Week, days getting longer, you land . . . in *Newark*.

The snow on the sidewalk, that clung to your sweatpants, is brown, in rain, then gone.

Crossing the Hudson, you remember – a magician plans to float over it. Using only helium balloons.

Everything is possible. Still.

From your taxi window, rain sprinkles hot dog vendors and street performers.

You go direct – not to your hotel, but to – *him.*

You like him because he is different to anyone you've met in 'Art'.

The curators in Chelsea and Soho. The artists in Bed-Stuy.

Not talking about 'movers and shakers', and 'looking past big names'.

And you like him because he books cars for you, without asking first.

And nearing Brooklyn – you reflect you are approaching something near normal, fixed.

And though you live apart, still you feel:

the wind blow under the door.

Sunday night box sets.

Invitations 'home'.

From his apartment you see cherry blossoms start in Prospect Park.

As you make yourself unavailable, he cleaves closer.

Enter Ariel, coming back from work.

It all becomes a little:

Ariel (*enthusiastic*) How was your day?

Anna Are we doing that?

Ariel What?

Anna 'How was your day'.

Ariel We can . . . *not*? Do you not want to?

Anna (*to audience*) He is a moth to the flame of your unkindness.

Ariel . . . Anna?

Anna No, sure. We can order takeout and kill ourselves also. It will be quicker.

Ariel (*beat*) Okay. That's cool.

Anna Tell me what you *feel*. Not, like: *habitual*.

Ariel (*beat – smiles*) You really don't bullshit, do you?

Anna Hm?

Ariel You . . . continuously say it how you see it.

Anna How it . . . *is*?

Beat. He smiles at this.

Ariel I guess . . . you can spend so long being 'appropriate'. Not saying or doing what you actually: *want*.

Anna (*shrugs*) Pointless.

Ariel *Right?* (*Beat.*) So how was your day?

Anna Ariel.

Ariel Serious. I wanna know.

Anna I spoke to lawyers who were condescending.

Ariel Yeah? Problem?

Anna Cashflow issue. Is nothing.

Ariel 'Kay . . . What else?

Anna Lunch with a Beijing collector at Sadelle's.

Ariel Yeah. How's the . . . *outlook?*

Anna New York is poised to eclipse London. We are . . . well placed.

Ariel Uh-huh. What d'you do for fun?

Anna I looked at the blossom in the park from your top window. Any other questions?

Ariel You could see it all the time if you spent more time here.

Anna Ariel.

Ariel What?

Anna Your apartment is not the only place in New York I can see blossom.

Ariel . . . I shouldn't bring up . . . *the pedestrian.*

Anna Not at all.

Ariel Kill myself instead. Got it.

2

Anna And one day – bright, cold – you deign to walk with him through Brooklyn.

And hiking through Green-Wood Cemetery, white jet marks in blue sky –

Ariel catches up, blowing his hands for warmth.

Ariel I cannot get over how *crisp* it is. So . . . *crispy*, y'know?

Anna Your first fight.

Ariel So: *seasonal.*

Anna First obstacle.

Ariel Reminds me of walking back home in the Midwest. We used to hike out to this water tower. Panoramic . . .

Anna His cheer irrepressible.

Ariel You walk as a teenager? In Russia?

Anna With headphones, sure.

Ariel The best.

Anna No it was totally *boring*.

Ariel Really? (*Beat.*) This is great though, right? Look at these guys: mausoleums, angels, urns. Decadence of it.

Anna (*shrugfully*) It's okay.

Ariel Like that one?

Anna Which?

Ariel Weird, Egyptian [one] – ?

Anna No way. Hate.

Ariel Really. That one?

Anna Absolutely hate.

Ariel Not a tomb fan, huh. Regular grave girl?

Anna Definitely not. Cremate me. (*Beat.*) My last hope for a smoking body.

Ariel Okay, hey now, you have a hot body.

He stops and looks at a gravestone.

Weird though. Huh? Knowing the first date, but not the second. Like: when is it gonna *be*?

Anna (*a little derisive*) Least you know what name will be on yours.

Ariel Huh. Fuck. (*Beat.*) That's actually very . . . profound.

Anna No it's not. It's obvious. Just you're a man.

Ariel Okay but . . . know what . . . *kinda* name you think you'd like, on there, perhaps?

Anna (*innuendo*) I like all kinds. All different sizes and shapes . . .

Ariel (*disappointed*) Gotcha . . .

Pause.

Why d'you do that?

Anna What?

Ariel Like: resist. Deflect.

Anna Deflect? What exactly?

Ariel I feel like you *reject* platforms for intimacy –

Anna Because I don't wanna talk about sharing names on a gravestone, c'mon –

Ariel Okay but – *not just*. Like: opportunities for affection.

Anna Ariel I have to travel again soon / [I don't wanna get into] –

Ariel *See*. This is it. That's what I mean. You're like a frickin' . . . (*Gesturing to sky*.) vapour trail, right? –

Anna

Ariel How many toothbrushes do you have in how many bathrooms? You come and go, right? I mean, did someone hurt you, or . . .?

Anna (*mock cry face*) Yes, Ariel, *someone hurt me* and now I retreat from relationships. It's so really *sad*.

Ariel (*pause – shrugs*) Right, mock, sure. But I feel like . . . you build a wall of irony around yourself / sometimes . . .?

Anna (*mocking*) 'A wall of irony'? I think you misunderstand irony.

Ariel Whatever. I mean: you make yourself a fortress. / Like when I bring up [moving in] –

Anna A fortress with a wall of irony built round it. And I'm inside that fortress? Seems like a mix of metaphors.

Ariel Yeah: forget it.

Anna Maybe you need a simple Midwest girl, Ariel. Girl next door . . .

Ariel What is *wrong* with you? I'm just trying to get close to you / here

Anna Know what? –

Ariel What?

Anna Fuck me in the mouth if you wanna get close to me. Don't talk.

　　Pause.

Ariel Really.

Anna

Ariel Know what, I'm gonna give us a minute.

Exit Ariel. Anna, alone.

Anna And in this moment you remind yourself:

Choose solitude. Choose to be alone on purpose.

Ariel re-enters.

Pause. A froideur between them.

Ariel Okay.

Anna So . . . I probably wanna go?

Beat.

Ariel I didn't bring this up before, and – I didn't say cos it was kinda random. But – did you use my name to extend a credit line? With Grigorian capital? Without telling me?

Pause. Anna shrugs.

Anna Sorry. What?

Ariel For your foundation.

Anna Excuse me?

Ariel Are you using me? I didn't think about it at the time but . . . did you say we were acquaintances, to meet their investment board?

Anna Ariel. I dunno. I meet *so many* firms.

Ariel Cos if you did it's no biggie. Just: I wanna know . . . where we're going with this. Like: am I being *paranoid*, or am I *useful* to you. Or *what*? Cos also . . . the thing with the hotel bill – ? I'm not *prosecuting* you but . . .

Anna (*rising irritation*) Oh my god I can pay you back for that. *Now*, if you want / I said.

Ariel I'm not saying that. I just: I wanna *know*, y'know?

Anna Know *what*?

Ariel (*points to himself*) And listen, I'm *a tombstone*, okay? Nothing goes further, I swear.

Anna You're saying *I lied*? Am *lying* – what?

Ariel I just wanna know *who you are*. Okay? Y' know?

Anna Ariel, what are you *saying*. Speak: *English*.

Ariel Okay this time, truly. Level with me. (*Beat.*) Cos I got industry people asking about you. But you have your trust. But *then* I hear you're trying to raise a loan through Grigorian? However then – *then* you tip our driver here a fuckin' Benjamin? So I'm thinking, I need to work this out. Cos money – money is easy, right, Anna. Isn't it? I think? So there's something else. Right? Going on. Is there not?

So I'm asking you – about: *you*. What is going on? With *you*.

   Silence.

Anna (*quiet*) Me. (*Beat.*) Okay.

   She nods to herself.

Okay.

   Pause.

Once upon a time there was a girl – and this girl –

Ariel Wait, what. What is this?

Anna Once upon a time, there was a girl. Yes?

   Beat.

This girl.

She met a man.

[She was very beautiful.]

55

She came from a far-off place.

And what you need to know about this girl is, she had the finest silks and embroideries.

She went to all the best parties.

Everyone thought she was perfect.

Especially this man.

Even though.

Even though, um –

She was kind of scary.

Ariel 'Kay . . .

Anna puts a finger either to his or to her own lips.

Anna And this girl, she wore – like – a ribbon round her neck.

And she never took it off.

It was like kind of . . . a choker.

Anyway.

The man fell in love with the girl.

He loved her very much.

And he proposed to her.

Eventually, she said yes.

And on their wedding night, the man said:

Hey.

Why, please, do you have this ribbon round your neck?

Can you take it off?

And the girl said:

No.

I can love you, I can do anything for you, but I can never, ever take this ribbon off. Ever.

And the man said . . .

Okay.

So then, okay, the years passed.

And every year the man asked, can you take it off, please, we have no secrets.

And the woman said no, always.

Every year, no.

And the more she said no, the more he asked.

And the years passed, and every year they were happy.

But one day, the man said,

Please,

Now that we have loved each other, a very long time, please – please – may you take off your ribbon.

And the woman said if you have to, if you must, I will take it off. For you.

The girl began to untie it

And she said to him:

Now you will see

Why I could not take it off before.

And slowly and carefully

She untied the ribbon

And when she unwound the last thread

Her head . . . fell . . .

off.

Beat.

Do you like it? Do you like this story, Ariel.

Beat.

Ariel Um, I like hearing you tell it. Yeah.

Anna But did you understand it?

Ariel Maybe . . . no?

Pause.

Anna Everyone has . . . a past. Everyone has . . . something.

You like me how I am.

Right now?

Yes?

Beat.

Ariel Of course.

Anna So that's it.

Ariel That's it?

Pause.

You know . . . whatever it is – it's, like, safe with me, right?

Anna Yes.

Pause.

Ariel Wanna talk . . . more?

Anna No.

Ariel No?

Anna I'm going to buy cigarettes.

Anna looks at him affectionately, then leaves.

3

Ariel, alone. He sits.

Ariel (*to audience*) And if you're asking:

If I questioned: what that was . . . about, *exactly*?

Sure very much so.

But she had a point.

No one owes you their past.

'The heart of another is a dark forest – always.'

And it's not like Anna didn't *pay for stuff*.

Dinner. Trips. Tipping like a lunatic.

Money always appeared.

Anna appears.

Anna Hey. You ready?

Ariel Two months later. In a cab to Park Avenue.

Anna Never Uber. Yellow cab only.

Ariel Going to see Anna's building for the first time.

[By which I mean, *I* was visiting for the first time.] Between meetings with architects and hedge fund managers –

Anna [So much bullshit, I'm sorry.]

Ariel – She'd fitted me in. And this place, I'm not kidding you. It was – like Amsterdam. Y'know? Flemish. Five stories. Ornate. (*To Anna.*) [Is this what the architecture is like in Moscow?]

Anna [Absolutely not.]

Ariel And in a mirrored elevator on the way up: (*To Anna, in the mirror.*) You not nervous?

Anna No. Should I be?

Ariel My bowels always judder for these things.

She smiles.

Anna Wanna know my secret?

Ariel For the pitch? Sure. Why not.

Anna examines him. They continue looking at each other in the mirror.

Anna One. Stand in the mirror. Often.

Ariel (*smiles*) Okay. Tick.

Anna Two. Every conversation has a winner and loser.

Ariel Okay. Who's winning now?

Anna Three. Don't be amazed by anything. Ever. Joy, despair: these are excessive emotions.

Ariel For you maybe.

Anna Four. The world wants to be deceived. Give them what they want.

Ariel Uh, really?

Anna Five. Don't contend with someone who has nothing to lose.

Ariel Scary.

Anna And six.

Ariel Six?

Anna If all else fails, cry.

Ariel Yeah? You think?

Anna (*beat – shrugs*) Maybe.

Ariel Those are pretty good. Where d'you get 'em?

Anna All over.

Beat.

Ariel So not nervous.

Anna It doesn't matter whether I am or not. I don't show it.

She kisses him, passingly, then goes out of the elevator without him.

Ariel And man did we get a welcome. Real estate in Manhattan? No joke. Agent was obsequious to the point of nausea. And while Anna spoke to investors –

Anna Post-War and Contemporary is the Market's primary locomotive.

A Warhol sold for *thirty-seven million* in Christie's evening sale last night.

Ariel I looked round. (*To Anna.*) And, Anna – this place is *amazing*. The views over the Hudson, high ceilings–

Anna A palace of glass and space.

Ariel (*to Anna*) Hirst?

Anna Me.

Ariel Nice. How did it go with the investors?

Anna They don't understand.

I want to make something incredible – like Moscow's metros.

Columns, marble, chandeliers.

Ariel You'll have to take me.

Anna I will.

Ariel It sounds great.

Anna I'm so close.

Ariel To what?

Anna *This! My foundation!*

Ariel You're so impressive. I wish I could be part of it.

Anna Shut up.

Beat.

Ariel Serious!

Anna Ariel, shut up. This is not what *this* – (*She means their relationship.*) *is.*

Ariel I know but . . . if your inheritance is delayed. Anna, I'm here . . . Y'know . . . ?

Anna Really?

Ariel Yeah! I think so?

Anna But – you want to?

Ariel I mean . . . (*Beat.*) Can I think on it?

He breaks away.

4

Anna And at times like this – in draughty buildings – you think back to your old life.

To the first time you learnt – how people come: *to you.*

You think of lecture halls in Goldsmiths University, parties in open warehouses.

When you are twenty-two, in final year, *failing.*

You study Fine Art.

You are nice to people but no one wants to be friends with 'foreign student'.

You have purple tints in your hair [of course].

You are in a lecture 'critiquing' the YBAs.

> *Lights change. The ambience of a darkened lecture.*
> *Totally eerie. After a moment Hirst's fly-killing strobes*
> *illuminate. An electrified fly guillotine.*

How they cannot paint, cannot draw, have only: concept.

You hear about Charles Saatchi arriving at a warehouse in a Rolls Royce.

Standing open-mouthed in front of a box containing a cow's head, maggots, and flies being killed by an electrocuting light.

The concept is: fear of death.

He buys it.

And you are thinking about this story – on a bus to a party that night in New Cross.

And about your end of term report that day.

It says Effort: Good. Achievement: Satisfactory.

And arriving at this party:

Of white walls, students smoking inside, a DJ in a living room – you realise:

Every night is ironic.

Ironic hip hop night.

Ironic acid trance night.

Ironic garage night.

What is even *true* or *now*?

And everyone is just so edgy by saying nothing.

And now –you are upstairs.

In a bathroom with an English boy called Conrad.

The bath is overflowing plastic. The boy says:

Conrad It's bubble wrap. Get it? A bubble bath.

Anna (*to audience*) You look at yourself in the mirror.

(*To Conrad.*) I get it.

Conrad I like your hair.

Anna Thanks.

(*To audience.*) He is gay. He eats out of the palm of your hand.

And then, watch this, it happens.

Conrad Hey – are you the Russian girl?

Anna Excuse me?

Conrad I heard there was a Russian oil heiress here worth, like, a lot of money.

Anna What's her name?

Conrad I don't know her name.

Anna (*to audience*) And at that moment: you decide you are *not* talentless.

You are not good at '*Fine Art*', but you understand the world, what people want. Concepts. Ideas. How to make a connection.

And you say:

(*To Conrad.*) You know, it's weird to think people who don't know you are talking about you at a party.

    Beat.

Conrad Fuck. Sorry.

Anna (*to audience*) It's that easy.

He brings you to his *parents' house*.

Conrad Notting Hill. Sorry, not the posh bit.

Anna There is *real art* on the walls. His parents –

Conrad They collect a little.

Anna And you talk all night. About plans.

Conrad *Fundamentally* changing the art scene.

   Anna smiles, looks up.

Anna Is that a Koons? Up there.

Conrad What?

Anna A Jeff Koons?

Conrad Oh. Right. Yeah, like it?

Anna Um.

I love it.

(*To audience.*) And you know then. Life can be better.

Conrad You going to Frieze?

Anna Maybe the after-parties, not the fair I don't think.

Conrad Mm. Vicious.

Anna And leaving the next day not having slept, you take Bus 148 back – forever – to Camberwell.

And in your room with no furniture and nothing on the walls, you open Instagram.

You look at the people you love.

Who make influence from nothing. Who make envy like currency.

And that day:

You go to Harrods. You take pictures of yourself in a Givenchy dress, which you shoplift, along with Celine sunglasses.

You go to the Mayfair galleries, you go to White Cube, Gagosian.

Damien Hirst retrospective at Tate.

    Beat.

Damien Hirst says: *You have to work with the tools of today.*

And so you use your phone to start a new beginning. You find photos of art you like.

On Instagram, you curate, @ your new friends. Learn power of association.

And when months later – you have stopped going to classes – this boy tells you about a magazine internship.

In New York.

His parents know the owners –

Conrad They could make an introduction.

Anna And you decide: yes.

    Beat.

And by the time you've landed in New York you will have committed.

You will buy bottle service at bars. You will have the best Instagram in the city.

Your story will become an advert for how far you can go by tipping.

And where you will meet a man, who offers you money without knowing even your name.

5

Lights and sound snap back to:

New York's skyscrapers are framed in the building's windows.

It is night and calm now.

Ariel reappears touches her.

Ariel Anna, I'm here . . . Y'know?

> *Beat.*

Anna Really?

Ariel Yes. I think so?

Anna But – you want to?

Ariel I mean . . . (*Beat.*) Can I think on it?

Anna (*closes her eyes/smiles*) Of course.

> *They turn and look out the windows together. Ariel takes in the space. They face away from us.*

Ariel Look at the size of this place. Listen to . . . the echo . . . Reminds me where we met. But . . . six storeys up everything is . . . *cleaner.*

> *Pause.*

Anna.

Anna Wait. Wait a second.

Ariel No I was gonna say –

Anna No, hold on a sec. Wait.

Ariel You okay?

> *She rests on him.*

Anna I like it. Here with you. Perfect quiet.

They look out at the buildings together. She takes his hand. They face away from us; she looks straight out.

You know . . . ?

Ariel What?

Anna We met at a very good time in my life, Ariel. In our lives.

He looks at her. She detaches.

Anna exits.

6

Ariel, alone.

Ariel One week later, she left town.

Had to reset her ESTA.

During that time, I take the app: *international.*

Developing markets.

And as I set off to travel, the pinnacle of my itinerary, okay, is a tech conference, in Beijing.

But this Beijing meet. Very much not my deal: A round-table 'Futurist-CEOs in Tech' thing. Lotta press.

So I was meeting with a journalist that morning. Ballbuster. *Fact-checker.* Gonna be a big *Forbes* profile. We meet at this Canton hotpot place for breakfast.

Lights change. A Canton diner. Twilight dawn. The sound of sizzling beef. The English journalist is officious and quietly probing.

Journalist (*ignoring him*) Shall we start with the figures?

Ariel Sure, for sign-up?

Journalist More like your revenues this year next to last. Recent investment –

Ariel No. No way. We're a private company, dude. That shit's all . . . off the table.

Journalist I really think the long-term viability of the product / is worth touching on –

Ariel They have aspirin here y'think? Look, just take it from me, the app is doing very well. (*Holds head in slight pain.*) You had figures about growth in the press pack, right?

Journalist Are you okay?

Ariel Fine. Just, look, I'm . . . *really* quite hungover. Like . . . there's a fan constantly going in my head or something . . .

Pause.

Journalist D'you want me to put that in the interview?

Ariel No. I just meant –

Journalist Well, let's get into the app then. Which I've had access to.

Ariel Oh you're on it?

Journalist No, I was put on it. I was given an account. By your people.

Ariel Well, great. You have a good time?

Journalist (*hesitates*) I mean, I saw a lot of good-looking people.

Ariel You were searching both?

Journalist Sexes? Sure. (*Beat.*) But the crowd leans straight, right?

Ariel Um, I'm not sure that's fair.

Journalist It's definitely fair. Can we go to some user reviews?

Ariel (*hungover answer*) Um. Yes?

Journalist So this is from a user I interviewed. We'll call him *Rick*.

(*Referring to notes.*) Rick will never forget his first Genesis date.

Ariel Uh-huh . . .

Journalist He met a woman at her million-dollar New York apartment, paid for by her father.

Rick told me:

'Within minutes, this woman had got naked, handed me her phone and asked me to photograph her.'

'The app's incredible,' Rick says.

Ariel (*shrugs*) I don't really see the problem. Sounds like they had a good time.

Journalist *Rick* did.

Ariel Man, come on, *what* – this is like . . . you just want your quote or whatever.

Journalist I have quotes. (*Beat.*) I guess, to *the point*: [what you created] this is a playpen for beauty snobs, right? Or: online frathouse-sorority for starfuckers? Like . . . your girlfriend?

Ariel Hey, what?

Journalist And there's nothing wrong with that. / Per se.

Ariel Um, you don't know the first thing about any of that, / I think –

Journalist But, I dunno. Like, sex as networking – have you considered that's what's on the table here?

Ariel (*beat*) Okay, listen. (*Beat.*) You want my justification? First dates have always been reveals, right? Like, does the person appear to match who they said they were on the internet? Are they as good looking? . . . Do they really work at Condé Nast? . . . Are they a creep? I wanted to *end* that period of scepticism. Now is there anything else pressing here, cos you seem to have an agenda –

Journalist Could I actually ask you another question about Anna?

Ariel Why? I thought this was about the app.

Journalist No, it will take that in, but – I was just interviewing another founder here. He started the Dream Catcher app, if you know it?

Ariel Um. No. Sounds fuckin' stupid.

Journalist

Ariel (*losing patience*) Fine, whatever. So?

Journalist Anyway, this guy said he knew Anna about a year ago. They toured art fairs . . . Her family is big in antiques . . .

Ariel Antiques? No her family is from oil.

Journalist Right, sure . . . Anyway, this guy pays her way round the world a couple of times. Considers investing in her foundation. But then, when he changes his mind and starts trying to recoup his money – he says he hears some pretty weird stories from her –

Ariel Hold on, is this article about *Anna*?

Journalist Tangentially.

Journalist disappears. It begins to snow.

Ariel And do I tell her about the time Anna skipped out on her hotel bill?

Or the fact I just gave her fifty grand of my money towards the lease on her gallery.

I do not.

And – meanwhile – I'm touching down in Sydney when this hits.

7

A phone call. Ariel takes it under the awning of the breakfast hotpot place, shivering.

Jed Grigorian Ariel, it's Jed from Grigorian.

Ariel (*a little startled*) Hey. Hey, Jed.

Jed Grigorian Are you awake?

Ariel Um, yeah. Yeah very much so.

Jed Grigorian Uh-huh. Captured the unicorn yet?

Ariel Working on it. I'm actually in Sydney right now. Just comin' up to 3.15 actually, in the a.m.

Jed Grigorian (*not listening*) Good. That's great. Ariel, I'm gonna cut to the crap.

Ariel Mm. Let's do that.

Jed Grigorian Right. Are you aware of what's going on. In New York.

Ariel At Genesis. I'm sixteen hours out. What's up?

Jed Grigorian Have you spoken to Marcus?

Ariel He's not been in touch. Is everything . . . kosher?

Jed Grigorian Listen, Ariel, sounds like something's a little . . . wrong –

Ariel (*to audience*) And it becomes extremely clear *everything*, not *something*, is wrong. What started as a

72

'minor glitch' in onboarding – vetting new clients – first means no new applications are being processed – then, *suddenly*, *everyone* is allowed on. The vetting system is *broke*. All applications accepted *immediately*.

And, in New York, *no one* is picking up to me.

And at that moment – who do I get a call from, but –

Anna (*edge of panic*) Ariel?

> **Ariel** Anna,
>
> Hey.

Anna Hi

Long time . . . no speak

Where are you

I missed you

> **Ariel** Yeah
>
> Um
>
> I'm at an airport
>
> In Sydney

Anna Oh

That's nice

   Ariel About to get a twenty-one-and-a-half-hour flight

Anna Yeah?

You can watch so many movies

   Ariel I think I'm gonna be mainly programming, actually

Anna Ah

Neat

73

Ariel Anna, I'm kinda in the middle of a work . . . thing

Anna Could I see you?

                                        Ariel I'm

          I'm in a Departures lounge in Australia

                              What's going on?

Anna When you're back?

. . .

I um – I was wondering –

Would you make *um, another* investment?

[In my project?]

                    Ariel An investment. Ah –

Anna Or – an investment *in me?*

                      Ariel (*makes noise*) Um

Anna Or, like, a loan?

I'm having some cash-flow issues

. . .

                                Ariel Um

                                I already did

                          . . . and the hotel . . .

Anna I thought . . .

I thought we were having fun

                                Ariel Yeah

                                    Sure

          But: what's that got to do with it?

Anna I'm just –

I'm trying to do this *thing*, and it's really hard. You know?

Ariel Anna, I'm running a business

Anna . . .

So am I

Ariel . . .

Right

Anna I actually overdrafted my account

A little.

Ariel Can you call . . . your parents?

Anna They're not in the country

They're in Africa, I think

Ariel Um

Anna, my flight is boarding

I have to go

Anna Yeah, but like . . .

I didn't say this, but, I like you

I think I actually like you. Like for real

Like, I think I love you, like you

I mean I have no idea what those words mean

It's easy to lie in another language . . .

Like, in the past – 'I like you – I love you'

I don't know what other people mean when they say that

But

I thought I hated you

Ariel But you want me to give you money

Anna Yes

But

Only for a little bit

Until I get this –

> **Ariel** And, you think – what?
>
> You think *I'm* from the Hamptons
>
> You think I was born *with this*?

Anna You have connections

You're American

This is important

> **Ariel** Anna

Anna I'm in trouble

> **Ariel** I'm hanging up

Anna shouts 'Fuck', exits.

8

Ariel I fly American Airlines.

By the time I get to JFK . . . the company – is *tumbling*.

And arriving in an Uber to Williamsburg, I reflect that the value of the company – *my* company – is founded entirely on reputation.

(*Shouts.*) Marcus!

Marcus Dude.

Ariel And this gimp, this fucktard, this Princeton . . . *dickhole* –

Marcus Dude. Relax.

Ariel The update. How long's it gonna take?

Marcus – We just . . . struggled to find the problem.
Y'know? These things take a while –

Ariel How long?

Marcus (*quietly*) Um. (*Beat.*) Fifteen hours.

Ariel (*beat*) Fifteen . . . Are you *kidding me*? That's a
lifetime.

What the fuck *happened*?

Marcus Uh –

Ariel Do you understand? Am I speaking *in code*? In one of
the many fucking *languages* you *do not know*?

Marcus Um, man –

Ariel – You think it runs itself? You think it comes that
easy?

Marcus We thought –

Ariel Look out the window, you see the grid system?

You think, what? You think *God* designed that, you think it
happened by chance?

Marcus Ariel. Dude –

Ariel We *run* an *operating system. Everything* is an
operating system. It's your *job* to keep that *going*. That
continuity.

Marcus Man. *I'm sorry*. But –

Ariel But what? *What*?

Marcus Man, you *weren't here*. You took your eye off the
ball. *You* fucked the membership.

Ariel (*beat*) Excuse me?

Marcus Dude, you not seen Twitter?

Beat.

Ariel (*to audience*) And the same day – the fucking same day – the news broke:

Marcus '*Socialite scammer arrested on grand larceny charges*'.

Isn't this your girlfriend?

Ariel And . . . the *New York Post* had us pictured at Pace Gallery.

A long feature followed . . . '*Duped Tech CEO Boyfriend*'.

Beat.

And my recollection of the next day, the last day of May, was a dog, on the tracks of Williamsburg Bridge, delaying my subway home by an hour.

And the reason I remember this, is that I was on a journey back from an EGM with our investors in Manhattan.

Where I'd been told:

Brand value damaged.

Failing fast allows us all to move on quickly . . . and quietly.

Next time.

And just like that.

Warp-speed: from the next big thing yesterday, to yesterday's news today.

Anna So . . . I guess I could say . . .

I apologise for . . . the *mistakes* . . . I made?

Beyond that . . .

You criticise me for my actions. What they say about me.

   Pause.

My father said:

I was such a selfish character, that they couldn't do anything about it.

I was like that by nature.

   Beat.

So I guess you could say:

I'm not a good person.

And you should be yourself.

Authenticity isn't necessarily telling the truth.

And sometimes it's necessary for an individual to stand out from the crowd.

   Beat.

So I don't regret it.

As such.

And – sometimes, I sit in my room, in the rain of my humiliation publicly – and feel – really – (*Beat.*) *blessed.*

What I know is: It has been my great privilege to come to your country and speak your language and be accepted in your hearts.

Ariel I watched Anna's testimony – nine months later – from my parents' living room in St Louis.

I'd lost my apartment, I'd driven from the East Coast, and I didn't know when I was gonna be back.

She was facing three to eight years, having had a plea deal rejected.

The judge cited: lack of remorse.

And the charge sheet was impressive.

Fraud. Grand Larceny. Theft of Services.

All in pursuit of a loan that would never materialise, towards an arts foundation that would never exist.

She was one check away. From . . . legitimacy.

Not long after, an article appeared on Anna's story.

She was from Ukraine, not Russia.

Or France.

Her father was a truck-driver.

And as I read this article, I looked up Anna's Instagram.

It was still there. A mausoleum to a fake life.

The rain was steady out, news said court was adjourning for the day.

I switched on a video game that my brother had bought the year before.

It was a Western.

About a gang of outlaws, trying to outrun Modernity.

And I realised it was the game I'd wanted to make.

A vast, detailed, open world.

And I thought about America.

The Settlers heading out West, to make the world in their image.

That: insatiability.

And I thought . . . about *businesses*.

All those . . . *companies*.

Each with its story. Each with its once upon a time.

And I decided to visit Anna.

11

Lights change.

The buzz of a high security door, perhaps. The low-level lighting of a prison.

Anna So the building is sold?

Ariel It went to some Scandinavian guys making a photography museum.

Anna (*sighs*) Oh. What a shame. (*Beat.*) You could have come sooner.

Ariel You took my money.

Anna You wanted me to.

   Ariel smiles ruefully.

Am I still on Genesis?

Ariel You're still on. People don't really use it anymore, but you're still on.

Anna I have a lot of matches?

Ariel Oh yeah. You're a big deal now.

Anna Damien Hirst says: *What I really like is minimum effort for maximum effect.*

I like that.

Ariel You know, I always thought of Damien Hirst as more of a businessman than an artist.

Beat.

Anna Exactly.

Beat.

So the app is not a thing anymore?

Ariel Not really. It broke . . . my idea broke. I took my eye off the ball. I'm actually working on something new. (*Beat.*) Can I ask you something? Did you ever go to Moscow? St Petersburg.

Anna No. I've never been to Russia.

Ariel Not to the metro stations?

Anna Never.

Anna All the other stuff . . .

Anna Not as such.

Ariel (*nods head – almost impressed*) How is it, here?

Anna This place is not actually that bad.

Not that bad *at all*, actually . . .

I tend to see it as, um . . . a *zoological experiment*, kind of.

The people here are really fascinating.

There are murderers, and people who steal people's identities.

It's okay.

I go to the library. People treat books . . . carefully. Like . . . dishes.

Ariel You don't regret it? Like, any of it? I mean, didn't we . . . have something?

Anna That is a cliché.

Ariel Yeah? (*Beat – nods, smiles.*) Well, I was really enjoying it.

Pause.

Anna The night we met, I thought . . .

Ariel What?

Anna . . . things could be . . . (*Beat.*) I felt . . .

Ariel High?

Anna Different. (*Beat.*) But . . . everyone wants women to apologise.

Ariel Not saying . . . that.

Anna Of course not.

Ariel No, like, grand plan?

Anna Who says I don't have a plan?

The thing about this country is, it's a playground.

If *you* lie in America and it gets you where you *want*, you're an entrepreneur, not a criminal.

Pause.

But . . . the place *I'm* from – is like, one of the dark places on the earth.

It's cold, they have psychics, witches. It's hell.

Because what do we have?

Crimean wine, a flat economy, girls who dream of becoming surrogate wombs for American women.

We have iron ore. We have metal. We have coal.

And coal . . .

Coal, okay, does not want to be coal.

It wants to be diamond.

So if I could do it again? I would.

I would do it more.

Ariel Miss you . . . I think.

Anna You're deluding yourself. You miss the idea of me. The concept.

Ariel (*beat*) Isn't that, like, love?

Ariel makes to leaves. Anna stops him.

Anna D'you wanna play a game?

Beat.

Ariel Sure.

Anna Your turn or mine?

Ariel Yours.

Beat.

Anna My.

Ariel (*thinks*) . . . Unbearable?

Anna (*thinks*) . . . Snowflake.

Ariel . . . *Dream.*

Anna thinks for a few seconds.

Anna Okay. Period.

Ariel Period? What kind of sentence is that?

Anna . . . '*My unbearable snowflake dream*' . . . No, that's it. That's great. Perfect.

End.